the drunken psalms

samantha hauff

BookLeaf
Publishing

Presentation by *BookLeaf Publishing*

Web: www.bookleafpub.com

E-mail: info@bookleafpub.com

ISBN: 9789357440455

First edition 2023

to papa,

*you always told me i'd be a great writer, so
this first one is for you.*

*i hope your life in heaven is the bliss i
dream it is.*

till we meet again,

love, sammi

ACKNOWLEDGEMENT

To the talented and lovely, Emily Gervais—

A million thank yous for the cover art, for recreating my vision, and for calling my mind beautiful — I echo your sentiments back to you, tenfold. Emily is from Indiana and is a college student at Purdue University where she studies Russian and Naval Science. She has been doing art of many mediums for as long as she can remember, and is damn good at it. She is also a former wrestler and a current badass among mere mortals.
Keep up with her art! @ jupiterinthewintertime

All artwork from this book is hers and the rights to her work are reserved. So don't even think about it, you dirty little thieves.

PREFACE

to this book,

i wrote a letter to you
then cut it into paper dolls,
I can't decide if i should hide it in my
floorboards
or hang it on my walls

i pin rugs to my ceilings,
and screw ceiling fans to the floor

you make me completely and utterly
nonsensical.

new age tower of babel

God died alongside the stream under the
intersection bridge,
His ashes are the yellow daffodils;
proving He was here

His soul is the lone finch on the dying
deciduous;
living a breathing façade of death

man killed God and encased His body in a
concrete jungle

—modernity has murdered our spirits

the dissonance

i want to wear socks in the rain
and crawl on asphalt with bare knees.

i want to lie naked in a bed of snow;
i want to feel things i know i'll hate feeling.

i want to be six and fall off my bike for the first
time again.
i want to watch my mother kiss my raw elbows,
that was the last time i knew what love felt like.

in my dreams, i lie in papa's bed again and cry,
for a person and a place who now cease to exist.

and i'd pay all my pennies to buy another
moment of your time
but heaven doesn't bargain,
and i know not to play cards with God.
if there's a dealer, He shuffles the hand.
you'll get the short end of the stick, so deal with
what you're dealt;
i'm still understanding feelings i don't know if i
ever felt.

i'm asking God for forgiveness for things i've
never done but wish i did,
He knows i'd probably sell my soul off to the
highest bid.

still,

i forget i'm someone's child
and i grieve for people i've never met and places
i've never been.

—God, the bottoms of my feet feel so far from
the top of my head

for-profit prophets

enemies heads shattered by babe hand,
angels and virgins scream, "how great thou art"
with their hymnal tongues twisted and
bloodshot'd eye—
at a candlelit service filled with folks i hadn't
seen since easter,
coming back for a victory lap at the foot of the
trough.
with their performative presents,
lacking frankincense and common sense

turtlenecks and neckties,
white lights blind a pseudo-baby in a manger,
today, heaven weighs a mere 8-pounds.

oh the holiest of nights,
i pray in a church parking lot:
God, mark up the price of salvation so high i
can't pay,
no better gift to give a king than my dignity.

marketeers playing God
to each i say,
"you're not a prophet if you're a slave to the
profit"

messiah sent,
holiday mint

keeping the 'Christ' in 'Christmas'
— easier said than done,
at least till April, when we chant:
"The grave has never won"

drunken custody

maryland motel,
you nursing a cigarette between your forefinger
and thumb.
baby sprite cans half replaced with vodka,
i fill mine with sugar just to watch it fizz.
empty mini mouthwash bottles and green food
coloring,
i know because your fingers are stained an eerie
color everest.

vices replace vices,
and crisis turns to crises

out of everything i know,
i best understand,

i'll spend my whole life trying to undo you.

—tell me what proof of liquor it takes to leave

baptist girl

bible belt born and bread,
oil anointed heads
highlighted verses,
and accidental curses
two girls from Sunday school,
even the Sabbath can't lay to rest
her dress touched her heels,
crosses dangled at her cheeks

—divine angelic feminine

when she held my hand to pray,
i didn't want to let go.
every night i longed to hold her and pray for
something true,
love letters to the Universe,
for a world where there's a 'me and you.'

wwjd bracelet on my left arm,
her, wrapped around my right.
i ask, "what would He do?"
i imagine He'd tell me to love, even if it's you.

she told me i am love, in the most biblical sense,
patient, kind, without envy, or boast.

—the girl i pray for most

her fingers tracing the inside of my palm as if
she's reading my future;
i clasp and squeeze as she rains blessings on my
shoulders.
cherish or perish,
and i choose the ladder

He is the way, the truth, and the light,
but she reflects light

— ethereal light

in my life, in my heart, on my mind, all the time.
she is sunlight in the dead of winter,
warming my skin.
i tell God, "the Sun shines if you let it,"
and You do.
and it is well.
and she is my sun,
and she is my moon,
and she is all my stars.
God, chart my constellations from afar.

as the galaxies worship Your name,
she proclaims all the kingdom's fame.
God's redeeming grace,
i catch a glimpse within her face.

the closer i draw to her, the closer i draw to Him.
so here I go, out on a whim—

— to my Boaz, my proverbs 31 woman, the
most equal yolk; triune and true
precious as rubies and just as rare
noble, virtuous, and free
it's not the most orthodox,
and they'll say my head's gone askew,
but God couldn't have given a person more
perfect for me than you.

if it's all mad—
i'd box up the love letters,
and let the prayers dissolve into words in the
sky.
but it's you,
and it's true,
it could never be bad.

baptist girl in this broken world,
let me lend a hand.
— to scarce to hold, we can't fit into their mold
but maybe, that's okay.
maybe they'll learn that someday

but for now,
i'll dry your eyes and fix your hair.
you fit into my perfect prayer,

unnamable,
untamable,
the words muster off my tongue:

— be my girl, be my one?

mirages and cigars

when the tea lit wicks turn black and stone cold,
woodwick we let turn to dust,
burning the midnight oil

— ephemeral

you're a smoke signal i followed far too long,
high over the trees i watch as you dissipate

without rhyme or reason,
without probable cause

leaving me to wonder where i went wrong,
left to a great wide somewhere

i have yet to trot

wondersome

your mediations and my one-off incantations,
revealed in the incandescent shimmer of your
mind;
silent spells cast with your hands

but there's truth in the unsaid,
is this a slow burn or am i burning myself out for
you?

—my meaningless matchbook

i saw the amber glistening in your eye,
your callused fingers smoldering my embers

somewhere etched between
the peace and the panic,
and the comfort and the chaos,
i stand on a tightrope of fear.

worried about never happened and
yets to happen,
happen-chanced side glances

i'd meet you for the first time a thousand times.

the corner of carl-bethlehem

they cut down the trees at the four-way by the
school,
i always wondered if you noticed things like
that.
maybe they got tired of cars wrapping around
trees and street signs alike,
of people too impatient for that prolonging red
light.

or maybe they'll build a duplex, high in the
sky—put this town 'on the map'
it'll be done in a year or two, or twelve;
but for now it looks like a red-dirt wasteland of
dry Georgia clay,
contrasted by mustard'd yellow machinery

but for now i sit at this red light,
for the five hundredth or five thousandth time
as a driver, a passenger, a friend, a lover, a
daughter

but this time i miss the trees i didn't ever expect
to miss,
and i miss moments etched into the ruby-haze
glimmering off my face.

i miss the corner of carl-bethlehem and the light
i prayed to be green when i was late to my first
period midterm,
or when i was rushing for no particular reason at
all,
just for the sake of living fast.

but i lived for those moments where i hoped the
red would never change,
where i reached for familiar hands nuzzling cold
6-speed shifters
and the same songs blazing out of old shoddy,
stock speakers.

maybe i don't miss the trees,
but rather the memories they witnessed.

the corner of carl-bethlehem and the side-street
hustlers
the locals'll swear are scamming you.
these rednecks and immigrants,
all chasing one thing:

comfort

i guess comfort can't come without change,
but change kills memories
and memories create homes,
i miss a place i can't identify and i've never
known

— this town is forever road work now

mason-dixon dreamer

i saw my mother kneel in a garden to harvest
squash and summer-ripe tomatoes,
it looked like earth was her altar.

sweat graced her forehead like dewdrops on a
muscadine,
a farmer's communion of homemade pie and
moonshine

southern-fried pollen stuck between the cracks
of the sidewalk,
folks with a slow drawl and a twang to their talk

pocket squares and cowboy boots,
i sow and reap all i have from my southern roots.

the coast is neither near nor far,
and dixie mommas'll spill your secrets over
sweet tea in a mason jar.

union boys and girls with expensive clothes,
drown their savings for youthful wedding oaths.

blue collars grow tight and suffocate dreamers,

they sink their sorrows in a PBR and pray to
their redeemer.

this melancholiac song of a working man,
i read chapter books off of a rough and calloused
hand.

'cause outlaws aren't born with a trust fund or
401Ks,
but rather with a smile and a story about the
'glory days.'

so meet me a road off from a prayer mile,
if you've nowhere to go,
sit, and stay awhile.

God, let me move as slow as a southern
stream—

the roses smell better when you have the time to
stop and dream.

sonnet to a sunrise

nothing can make a preposterous pigeon scream in the city, or a rural rooster crow
like the break of light can.
the dawn dawned on me as i prayed a solemn parting to the little lights
dancing around the crown of my head.
my church is the stars in the sky,
holes God poked in the Container
just so we can breathe.
how thoughtful He is,
we are the stick bugs and beetles collected in his Rubbermaid;
hiding under rocks.
He picks up one and blinds me
with hues of pink and orange.
beauty, forever steals my eyes
and like God— the Sun, never dies.

sonnet to a sunset

how fast do i need to drive to never see the sun go down?
i'm chasing these sunsets, these perfect sunsets,
but they're always running faster away than i am towards them.
it's this eternal peril of having the light of the world at your fingertips,
but not quite ever grasping it.
i feel like i'm always chasing the impossible–
the Divine and the holy.
but as i chase, i trip and fall on my knees
and watch the light of the world fall with me
and time chews on my temple
and tomorrow comes like a promise
and the day is done, warping into history.
but the only thing i can tell you about the fall is,
you can never hold a sunset.

this isn't about a sunset

heaven is the end of the
world

and i feel the end of the world creep up from the
shadows;
behind the trees that made no sound because no
one heard them fall,
behind my sack of bones that collapsed with
them all.
a blazing white horse and silver locks of royalty
accompany me,
trumpets sob in glory.

a sign a fore-right exit from mine yells,
'JESUS IS COMING'
now here i am, shaking His hand.
we sit down at the 4th corner of the earth to have
a chat.

and we argue about righteousness for
righteousness' sake,
i moan to Him about the people who spit bible
verses in my face.

He tells me of His trauma and shows me His
scars,
i show Him mine.

we trade war stories and with His voice, He
creates stars.

and we think about the times we thought we
were invincible,
times when we thought God couldn't touch us
—we were wrong

we ponder if God truly has any mercy;
He tells me about the gardens He wept in
because of the darkness His Father passed to
Him,
i echo His sentiments
and at our elbows, we interlock by the limb

we walk from the edge of the earth to its core,
i ask Him questions till my lips grow sore.
His feet are bare,
my footprints aren't there

and i'm used to people standing on my shoulders
to get a better look at someone else,
but He holds me on His and takes me to a grand
and broken mirror.
my reflection looks different, almost beautiful
a peace i've never felt floods me, it's so unusual
i ask Him who i look at;
she's strong, and healthy, and so incredibly kind.

He tells me she is everything i am but with a
softened mind.

—in that moment, all of heaven wraps me in its
arms

the light of the Sun burns out and goes dim,
still, there's nothing i wouldn't give to sit on the
corner of the earth for eternity with Him.

the end is here,
but i hold no fear;

i have learned heaven—
is just the freedom of my mind

fear no evil

a broken stained glass window i watched shatter
into my lap,
i collect the shards in a crystal jar
like sea glass weathered by God,
as a weapon i forge against my own flesh

those blood-letting vampires,
stuck between my two ears,
curse me for the indiscretions of my teenage
years.

old testaments test my patience,
mourning rites and my right to passage;
pagan gashes cut down to my bones.

how ironic,
a tattoo covers my scar;
ironic that it's evil i fear
—a drunken psalm imprinted in my skin

my sins betroth my sins,
in the holiest matrimony —
blood, finally runs white.

— read me Leviticus 19:28 again

men like to call me an old soul, it excuses their perversion

"you're so mature for your age,"
say the fingers suggesting under my chin to look up.
doe-like eyes,
our innocent embraces and sweet goodbyes
my girlhood tucked beneath a 'too short' skirt—
"make sure it's longer than your fingertips"

school girl,
cruel world
dirty men with eyes that unclothed me at 12

old souls with broken bones
beg denying pastor's wives
and their nepotistic police files

they call me a teenage stumbling block,
while brothers in Christ take a lap through town,
i can still hear his voice ring in my 14-year-old ear,
"take the ribbon out of your hair,
you're not as innocent as you want to appear."

your seminary degree and broken-spine'd
theology books can't save you from the
innocence you've stolen;
my teeth grind'd down and my eyes so swollen.

courtrooms declare you're a good man with a
few mistakes under your belt;
lucky you, your dead cop dad saved you from
pain i demanded be felt.

deacons who run this town sew my lips with
holy golden thread,
wash your hands clean, convince me it's all in
my head

but i don't hate you, though i wish i did.
my mother says hate is a strong word,
i think still not strong enough for this.

momma told me not to talk to strangers, i never
thought that meant youth ministers;
now the look on your face on the 'Bad and
Busted' page is something so, so sinister

God is a mother to me now, nurturing and kind,
She rubs my back and sweetly sings me to sleep.
the hands of the Divine hold me dearly, not
deathly

i run to the Mother, She brushes my hair with
quiet fingers.

i felt God move as you spoke and it terrified me,
lips that speak the gospel also chatter about my
adolescent curves.
i want to cut my body into a straight line so the
flesh you spoke about ceases to exist,
i wish tickets to heaven were voided for those on
the sex offenders list.

— God can't be a man, it would mean He has
something in common with you

plastic rosaries and $2 whores

the wrath of God

the grapes of God's wrath,
i bear fruit in my loins
from my chin to my hips,
a holy path

i feel my guts rearrange themselves in a single
file line,
the stairway to heaven is long and straight

mistress lips on a temple of a body,
this armistice of an unwedded woman

these virgin whores,
those celibate sluts

"you pray to God with those lips?"

yet,
platonic love wasn't enough

bible study

i'm looking for purpose in between the thinnest
fickle pages,
in leatherback prayers hidden in the seam of this
book.
i feel biblical angels set my hair on fire with the
heat of their tongues.

but i've got lion lungs of Judah,
—hear me roar
my proud and boastful soul is set ablaze,
by faith or by fear?
i think i fear my own faith.

a burning bush speaks to me in tongues,
i play double dutch with the devil
and i ballroom dance in a dress of fire
—i'm just hell's PlayPlace

a hot-breath'd whisper speaks to me:
"what a grim world,"
it's the devil on my shoulder,
shooting arrows at the angel at its polar.

i don't know if i believe there's a hell,
someone already taught it to me.

i've lived it, i've walked through it,
i've smelt it's scalding flames

i know Hell, but teach me God.

"in due time," a collar cherub whispers,
reading my mind.

a dove and a raven play tug-a-war in my head,
i tear out the pages of my Bible and tuck them
under the pillows in my bed.

i pray for sweet dreams and beautiful things
and sometimes,
during my nightly chats with the Divine,
i almost forget the could'ves
and i just live with what just is.

the path to the plan is straight through
acceptance and a stone-throw from grief

the least of these is a 10-year-old from Uvalde

"Truly I tell you, whatever you did for one of the
least of these brothers and sisters of mine, you
did for me." Matthew 25:40

i saw God get shot on the news today,
His reflection gleamed in a 5th grader's obituary
eye.
      —uvalde, texas

i saw the blood of a lamb lie on a congressman's
doorstep,
—an angry, mighty, wrathful lamb of God
he tweeted his thoughts and prayers and then
watched his hush money check clear.

i cried on the footsteps of a statehouse,
for children i had never known or met.
i screamed in the streets until i tasted blood in
my throat,
it tasted like pain and forgotten names.

i saw a mother cry,

i knew she remembered the first glance she saw
of her baby's eye,
not knowing the last thing that baby would see
was a dark, hollow gun barrel.
—a drive-by and a lifetime of maternal peril

i saw a crowd of people i preached to about
change,
i wonder if they're still in the right tax bracket to
remember my name.

i saw a Christian nationalist kill men and women
who loved like me,
how could we love the same God but he would
have me begging on my knee?

i heard a radio host ramble about his 'God-given
right to bear arms,'
how can you make a tragedy about yourself
when there's children at harm?
wanting teachers to go gun-toting above their
pay grade,
while the communal sensitivity to these deaths
just fade

my poetics and their politics,
hate me for calling out their propaganda cliques

black churches shot up by fundamentalists,

forgetting their 'white man's religion'
was ransomed, on a cross, by a colored man's
death.
false idols of a long-haired hipster white man,
dare i even waste my breath?
delusional nazis forget Jesus wasn't a skinhead,
His skin color wasn't mine, but His blood still
ran red.
   —charleston, south carolina

school zones shouldn't be war zones,
but teachers play heroes
when you can't get a cop worth a damn on the
phone.

and if you hate this poem, that's alright;
i read in the Good Book to fight the good fight.
bless'ed are the peacemakers, but how can there
ever be peace,
with student's constant bouncing legs and
ever-gritted teeth?

check your privilege at the door and i'll do the
same with mine,
hatred-filled white boys rhetorically excused for
their 'mental health' crime.
mental illness is global, but school shootings are
so American.

oh, and if a black man did it? well, let's look at
the comparison.
the news says white boys are 'just mental' but
black men are 'a danger,'
to me, they're all sick, sad excuses of men who
can't deal with anger.

just and merciful God, all i ask is why?
these empty graduation chairs sit so solemnly
awry,
these men and women,
these boys and girls,
lie dormant and cold.
while survivors still live crouched under their
desks,
praying to make it to 18-years-old.

if they didn't die then, they'll die there;
80-years-old and mentally still under that
classroom chair.

so if i die in English class, dump my ashes in the
schoolyard
and nail a note, like Martin Luther,
to the Senate's Chamber door,
with my own 95 Theses, all spelling out:

NOT. ONE. MORE.

i lost my wallet in purgatory

gasoline girls surround a friction fire
with flint stuck,
and smoky gut—
there's a boy praising God with a 40oz.

beauty,
is the chip on his shoulder;
they're singing gospel songs they'll forget the
words to when sober

this pow-wow at the edge of the earth,
debating the laws of the universe
and notions of rebirth

"throw another log on the fire, i could stay here
a while,"
says a girl with a beautiful gap to her smile.

it's windy by the river;
the air smells like sugar'd dirt,

i speak nonsensical words
about the symmetry of nature
and the askew of my mind,
with the brain of a bayonet;

in the distance,
i catch wind of folks smoking comically large
cigarettes.

i collect foreign money
and wage foreign wars between the gaps of my
teeth.
– 'show 'em your teeth, bulldog,'
so long as you still have teeth to show.

i've got teeth
and bones
and ribs as tough as rubber pellets,
safeguarding my philosopher's heart
and my troubadour soul

i kiss death goodnight;
i stand on the ashes of my burnt bridges,
and know
at the core
and at the marrow of me,
i'll never grow old.

i hope you find what you're looking for in the
very deepest parts of me

belief is a two-way street

i spend my nights in a dark room talking to a
blank page,
hoping the words i spit on it speak back.

these prayers of a poet,
these ballads to a God
who i spend my days convinced doesn't believe
in me back

a God i feel i'm just beginning to know
i still fall on my knees every night,

worshiping,
pleading to—

The Great Unknown

midwest intellect

illinois farmhouse,
grain cylinders and windmills shatter the clouds.
American flags and calls for revival,
savior found in the scarred hands of a child.

frozen lakes too thin to skate on—
i throw the boulders
weighing down my shoulders
at the icy sheet just to watch it crack

the birds flock south in jagged-shaped triangles;
their arrows point me home.

i want to live in a red house in a place that
doesn't exist,
write poems describing every hue of gray the
sky is;
i paint in watercolors but only see in black and
white

i want God to inhabit my feet and let me run
without growing faint,
inhale foggy toxins and not fear death,
lungs painted in grayscale and a snowy breath

i see rain in the distance and heaven peaks out
from the clouds,
it crystallizes and crashes into my cheek,
          i've never heard snow fall this loud.

i think God lives in my lungs and forces them to
heave.
if it was up to me, i'd choose not to breathe.
— it's so tiring being alive when your body
wishes it wasn't

when i go, i wanna bleed out in a snowy field;
it looks like a lovely place to die.

in between the raked imprints from the sowed
crops,
i'll let our secrets die and bleed out in a midwest
town with no name.

steel skylights will speak in morse code
to let the Universe know, i'm headed home

— i own everything that hurts

a golden prayer

so, in pursuit of treating others the way I wish to
be treated, if i fail, let me do so in love.
if i err, let it be with intentions of love.

let me continuously and endlessly extend
compassion towards others, even if they do not
extend compassion towards me.
let me love this earth and its inhabitants as my
divine creator has done for me.

let me embrace the undeniable
interconnectedness of life and add positivity to
its continuum.

—in all things, let me love as gracefully as i
have received love.

amen.

www.ingramcontent.com/pod-product-compliance
Lightning Source LLC
Chambersburg PA
CBHW070611160726
48003CB00005B/2218